THE OFFICIAL CELTIC ANNUAL 2021

Written by Joe Sullivan
Designed by Chris Dalrymple

A Grange Publication

© 2020. Published by Grange Communications Ltd., Edinburgh, under licence from Celtic Football Club. Printed in the EU.

Photographs by Alan Whyte and Ryan Whyte, Angus Johnston, Celtic Multi-Media, SNS Group.

Celtic logo is a registered trademark of The Celtic Football Club.

ISBN 978-1-913034-90-0

CONTENTS

CLUB HONOURS

Scottish League Winners [51 times]

1892/93, 1893/94, 1895/96, 1897/98,
1904/05, 1905/06, 1906/07, 1907/08,
1908/09, 1909/10, 1913/14, 1914/15,
1915/16, 1916/17, 1918/19, 1921/22,
1925/26, 1935/36, 1937/38, 1953/54,
1965/66, 1966/67, 1967/68, 1968/69,
1969/70, 1970/71, 1971/72, 1972/73,
1973/74, 1976/77, 1978/79, 1980/81,
1981/82, 1985/86, 1987/88, 1997/98,
2000/01, 2001/02, 2003/04, 2005/06,
2006/07, 2007/08, 2011/12, 2012/13,
2013/14, 2014/15, 2015/16, 2016/17,
2017/18, 2018/19, 2019/20.

Scottish Cup Winners [39 times]

1892, 1899, 1900, 1904, 1907, 1908,
1911, 1912, 1914, 1923, 1925, 1927,
1931, 1933, 1937, 1951, 1954, 1965,
1967, 1969, 1971, 1972, 1974, 1975,
1977, 1980, 1985, 1988, 1989, 1995,
2001, 2004, 2005, 2007, 2011, 2013,
2017, 2018, 2019.

League Cup Winners [19 times]

1956/57, 1957/58, 1965/66, 1966/67,
1967/68, 1968/69, 1969/70, 1974/75,
1982/83, 1997/98, 1999/00, 2000/01,
2005/06, 2008/09, 2014/15, 2016/17,
2017/18, 2018/19, 2019/20.

European Cup Winners 1967
Coronation Cup Winners 1953

NEIL LENNON

NEIL Lennon is synonymous with silverware success at Celtic Park, both as a player and manager as well as being involved in both capacities in some of the club's most successful European forays this Millennium.

Season 2019/20 was no different as the Hoops maintained their record of sweeping up on the domestic scene as well as recording a competitive European win on Italian soil for the first time ever - adding to achievements such as Seville in 2003 as a player and leading the side to the famous win over Barcelona in 2012 as manager.

The Irishman realised his Bhoyhood ambition when fellow countryman, Martin O'Neill brought him to the Hoops in 2000 and the battling midfielder maybe thought he had reached a pinnacle with the club he had always supported when he was made Celtic captain five years later in 2005…

That scenario would be decidedly overshadowed though as, not only would Neil Lennon go on to manage the club, but he would join club legend, the mighty Billy McNeill, as a captain who would not only manage the club, but like Cesar, would return for a second spell as manager and lead the club to even more silverware success.

In season 2019/20 he lifted the Scottish Football Writers' Association Manager of the Year award, the third time the Irishman has achieved that accolade, and it was awarded in recognition of another marvellous season for Neil Lennon at Celtic Football Club.

In leading the club to its second nine-in-a-row, Neil Lennon collected his TWENTIETH winner's medal as a Celt, and there aren't many people who have that claim to fame.

A lot has happened since Neil Lennon first walked through the doors of Celtic Park around 20 years ago as a player on December 6, 2000, and the story is far from over.

MANAGER FACTFILE

D.O.B:
25/06/71

Born:
Lurgan, Ireland

Playing career record:
Manchester City (1989-90),
Crewe Alexandra (1990-96),
Leicester City (1996-2000),
Celtic (2000-07),
Nottingham Forest (2007-08),
Wycombe Wanderers (2008).

Playing honours:
Leicester City: League Cup Winners
(1996/97, 1999/00).

Celtic:
Scottish Premier League Champions:
(2000/01, 2001/02, 2003/04,
2005/06, 2006/07).

Scottish Cup Winners:
(2001, 2004, 2005, 2007).

Scottish League Cup Winners:
(2000/01, 2005/06).

UEFA Cup Runners-up:
(2002/03).

As Manager:
Hibernian:
Scottish Championship (2016/17).

Celtic:
Scottish Premier League Champions
(2011/12, 2012/13, 2013/14,
2018/19, 2019/20),

Scottish Cup (2010/11, 2012/13,
2018/19), League Cup (2019/20).

CELTIC'S GOAL OF THE SEASON 2019/20

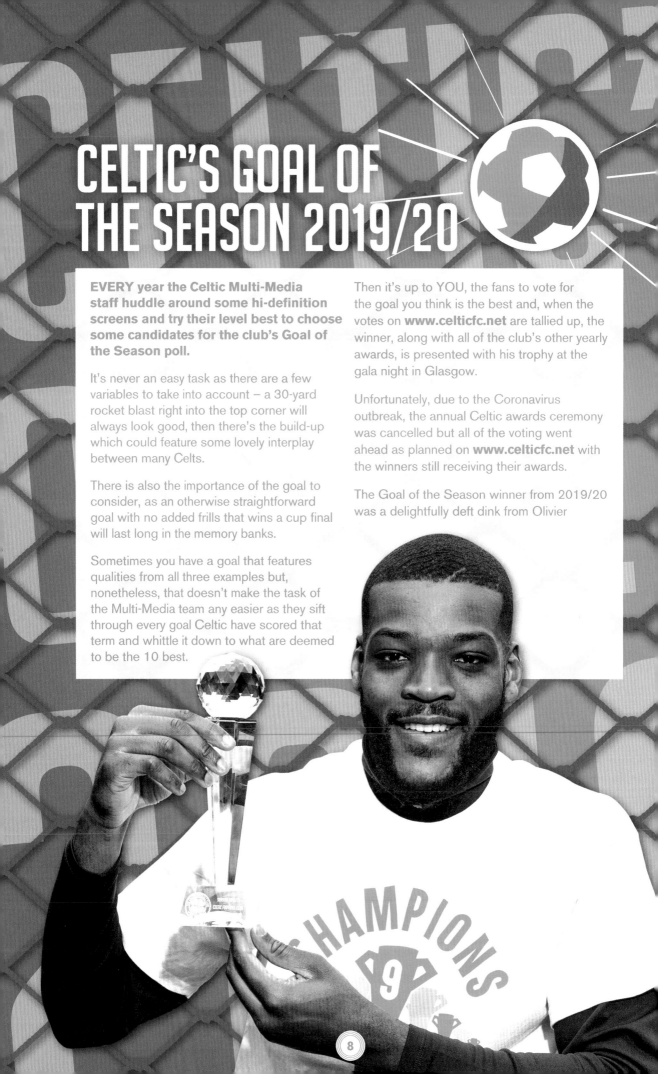

EVERY year the Celtic Multi-Media staff huddle around some hi-definition screens and try their level best to choose some candidates for the club's Goal of the Season poll.

It's never an easy task as there are a few variables to take into account – a 30-yard rocket blast right into the top corner will always look good, then there's the build-up which could feature some lovely interplay between many Celts.

There is also the importance of the goal to consider, as an otherwise straightforward goal with no added frills that wins a cup final will last long in the memory banks.

Sometimes you have a goal that features qualities from all three examples but, nonetheless, that doesn't make the task of the Multi-Media team any easier as they sift through every goal Celtic have scored that term and whittle it down to what are deemed to be the 10 best.

Then it's up to YOU, the fans to vote for the goal you think is the best and, when the votes on **www.celticfc.net** are tallied up, the winner, along with all of the club's other yearly awards, is presented with his trophy at the gala night in Glasgow.

Unfortunately, due to the Coronavirus outbreak, the annual Celtic awards ceremony was cancelled but all of the voting went ahead as planned on **www.celticfc.net** with the winners still receiving their awards.

The Goal of the Season winner from 2019/20 was a delightfully deft dink from Olivier

Ntcham that, apart from being a wonderful goal in its own right, also made Celtic history as the club had never won a competitive game on Italian soil, but that was all to change on the night of November 7, 2019. Neil Lennon's side came from behind to beat top Serie A side, Lazio, 2-1 in the Stadio Olimpico, and it was Ntcham who provided the injury-time winner for the Hoops.

Odsonne Edouard intercepted a pass out of the Lazio defence and pushed forward with Mo Elyounoussi and Ntcham in support. He opted to roll the ball into the path of his fellow countryman, who had come on in the 77th minute as a substitute.

His first touch was almost too far in front of him, but it actually provided the perfect angle for him to chip the ball over Lazio keeper, Thomas Strakosha, and into the net, sending 10,000 Hoops fans in the Rome stadium into raptures and creating Celtic history.

The scorer said: 'Before I came on, the manager said to me, try to defend a little bit, press when possible and when we get the ball, try to play forward and keep the ball. It was a difficult angle, but it happened too quickly to explain.

The other nine contenders were:

Leigh Griffiths v St Mirren
March 7, 2020

Callum McGregor v Motherwell
February 5, 2020

Olivier Ntcham v Partick Thistle
September 25, 2019

Odsonne Edouard v Rangers
September 1, 2019

James Forrest v AIK
August 29, 2019

Mikey Johnston v Dunfermline
August 17, 2019

Kristoffer Ajer v Motherwell
August 10, 2019

Ryan Christie v St Johnstone
August 3, 2019

Mikey Johnston v FK Sarajevo
July 9, 2019

THE 9-IN-A-ROW SEASON

CHAMPIONS

JULY

CELTIC kicked-off their pre-season work-out in Austria and Switzerland with two games at the end of June, clocking up a 6-1 win over SC Pinkafeld and a 2-1 defeat of Wiener SC before finishing off the trip with a 0-0 draw against FC St Gallen at the start of July.

That set the Hoops up for their competitive start to the term, but there would still be one more friendly game to play between the first two European ties, but that 0-0 draw with Stade Rennais to finish off the pre-season routine wouldn't be the last time the clubs would meet in 2019.

JULY FIXTURES

(Home fixtures in bold)

9	UCL	3-1 v FK Sarajevo (Johnston, Edouard, Sinclair)
17	**UCL**	**2-1 v FK Sarajevo (Christie, McGregor)**
24	**UCL**	**5-0 v Nomme Kalju FC (Ajer, Christie 2, Griffiths, McGregor)**
30	UCL	2-0 v Nomme Kalju FC (Kulinitis og, Shved)

Those first two games were against FK Sarajevo in the UEFA Champions League qualifiers and, with Mikey Johnston scoring the first competitive goal of the season, wins of 3-1 and 2-1 gave the Hoops a healthy 5-2 scoreline over the Bosnia and Herzegovinian champions.

Next up were Nomme Kalju of Estonia, and the home win of 5-0 was followed up by a 2-0 victory on the away journey for a 7-0 aggregate win to set the Hoops up for the league opener a few days later.

AUGUST

ASIDE from a sterling start to the league campaign, the month of August saw progress in the defence of the League Cup and an exit from the Champions League, but also qualification for the group stages of the UEFA Europa League.

It was a 5-4 aggregate defeat to CFR Cluj of Romania that closed the Champions League door, but a fine 6-1 two-legged victory over AIK of Stockholm put the Hoops into the Europa League group stages once more, while it was tight against Dunfermline in the League Cup with extra-time being needed for the 2-1 win over the Fife side.

AUGUST FIXTURES
(Home fixtures in bold)

3	**SPFL**	**7-0 v St Johnstone (Johnston, Christie 3, Ntcham, Edouard, Griffiths)**
7	UCL	1-1 v CFR Cluj (Forrest)
10	SPFL	5-2 v Motherwell (Ajer, Griffiths, Forrest, Edouard, Christie)
13	**UCL**	**3-4 v CFR Cluj (Forrest, Edouard, Christie)**
17	**LC**	**2-1 v Dunfermline (Johnston, Forrest)**
22	**UCL**	**2-0 v AIK (Forrest, Edouard)**
25	**SPFL**	**3-1 v Hearts (Berra og, McGregor, Bayo)**
29	UCL	4-1 v AIK (Forrest, Linner og, Jullien, Morgan)

It was all guns blazing in the SPFL, though, with 15 goals scored in the first three games and Flag Day getting off to the best of starts with a magnificent 7-0 win over Ross County and Ryan Christie netting a hat-trick.

Motherwell scored the first and last goals in the next league game at Fir Park, but the Celts netted five times in between those goals for a 5-2 win, and that was followed up by a 3-1 home win over Hearts, featuring a returning Fraser Forster who joined on loan from Southampton.

THE TOP 3

	P	W	D	L	F	A	GD	Pts
Celtic	3	3	0	0	15	3	12	9
Rangers	3	3	0	0	9	2	7	9
Livingston	4	2	2	0	8	4	4	8

THE  -IN-A-ROW SEASON

SEPTEMBER

WHAT better way to start a new month than by coming out on top in a Glasgow derby at the home of your rivals?

That's exactly what Celtic did at Ibrox on the first of the month as Odsonne Edouard got the ball rolling just after the half-hour mark, and Irishman, Jonny Hayes added the cream to the cake in the final minute to make it 2-0.

SEPTEMBER FIXTURES
(Home fixtures in bold)

1	SPFL	2-0 v Rangers (Edouard, Hayes)	
14	SPFL	1-0 v Hamilton Accies (Forrest)	
19	UEL	1-1 v Stade Rennais (Christie)	
22	**SPFL**	**3-1 v Kilmarnock (Edouard 2, Christie)**	
25	**LC**	**5-0 v Partick Thistle (Bayo, Rogic, Ntcham 2, Sinclair)**	
28	SPFL	1-1 v Hibernian (Christie)	

The rest of the month went unbeaten as well, although there were a couple of drawn games in there – both finishing 1-1.

The first of those, away to Rennes in France could easily have been a win for the Celts, but the outcome still gave the Hoops hope of further positive scores in Group E of the UEFA Europa League.

The other 1-1 tie was also away, this time to Hibernian at Easter Road in the SPFL, and that followed on from taking full points against Hamilton Accies away and Kilmarnock in the East End of Glasgow.

There was one more derby, this time against Partick Thistle in the League Cup, and the Hoops registered a 5-0 win to take them through to the semi-final.

THE TOP 3

	P	W	D	L	F	A	GD	Pts
Celtic	7	6	1	0	22	5	17	19
Rangers	7	6	0	1	21	5	16	18
Motherwell	7	4	1	2	13	10	3	13

THE 9-IN-A-ROW SEASON

OCTOBER

CELTIC'S Euro hopes were given a real shot in the arm with two great results at home over the course of the month with earlier foes, CFR Cluj, and Italian Serie A side Lazio, both falling to the Hoops at Celtic Park.

Goals from Odsonne Edouard and Mohamed Elyounoussi gained some retribution over Cluj for the Champions League exit earlier in the season, but even that was eclipsed by the visit of Lazio with the Celts coming from behind to take the game.

OCTOBER FIXTURES
(Home fixtures in bold)

3	**UEL**	**2-0 v CFR Cluj (Edouard, Elyounoussi)**
6	SPFL	0-2 v Livingston
19	**SPFL**	**6-0 v Ross County (Elyounoussi 2, Edouard 2, McGregor, Forrest)**
24	**SPFL**	**2-1 v Lazio (Christie, Jullien)**
27	**SPFL**	**4-0 v Aberdeen (Edouard, Frimpong, Forrest, Elyounoussi)**
30	**SPFL**	**2-0 v St Mirren (Elyounoussi, Forrest)**

Ryan Christie equalised with his 12th goal of the season, Christopher Jullien scored a last-gasp winner and Fraser Forster pulled off some world-class saves to leave Celtic unbeaten in the group.

In the league, there was a surprise 2-0 defeat on the artificial surface at Livingston, but that was followed by 12 goals to no reply in the next three SPFL outings. Ross County were dispatched 6-0 while Aberdeen were defeated 4-0 at Pittodrie with Jeremie Frimpong netting his first Celtic goal in only his third game.

The month finished with a 2-0 win over St Mirren as the Hoops maintained their position at the top of the table.

THE TOP 3

	P	W	D	L	F	A	GD	Pts
Celtic	**11**	**9**	**1**	**1**	**34**	**7**	**27**	**28**
Rangers	11	9	1	1	33	5	26	28
Motherwell	11	6	1	4	18	16	2	19

THE 9-IN-A-ROW SEASON

NOVEMBER

THE new month couldn't have gone any better for Celtic as they sealed European football after Christmas with games to spare, progressed to their fourth League Cup final in a row and took full points in both SPFL matches.

Both European games had tales to tell as a first competitive win on Italian soil ever, thanks to a last-minute strike from Olivier Ntcham leading to a 2-1 victory and meant Celtic were assured of qualifying from the group.

NOVEMBER FIXTURES
(Home fixtures in bold)

2	LC	5-2 v Hibernian (Elyounoussi 2, McGregor, Brown 2)
7	UEL	2-1 v Lazio (Forrest, Ntcham)
10	**SPFL**	**2-0 v Motherwell (Edouard, Tait og)**
23	**SPFL**	**4-0 v Livingston (Edouard, Brown, Forrest 2)**
28	**UEL**	**3-1 v Stade Rennais (Morgan, Christie, Johnston)**

The next European game saw the Hoops guaranteed first place with another match yet to go as the side defeated Rennes 3-1, with the French side getting a consolation goal right at the death.

The month started, though, with a trip to Hampden as Scott Brown scored a double against his old side in a 5-2 League Cup semi-final defeat of Hibernian to go through to a final date with Rangers.

No goals were lost in the league meetings as the Hoops beat Motherwell 2-0 and then maintained their eight-game winning run with a 4-0 defeat of Livingston – the last side to beat the Hoops.

THE TOP 3

	P	W	D	L	F	A	GD	Pts
Celtic	13	11	1	1	40	7	33	34
Rangers	13	11	1	1	38	8	30	34
Aberdeen	15	8	4	3	23	17	6	28

DECEMBER

THERE was no doubting the high point of the early part of the month as Celtic made it TEN trophies in a row thanks to four League Cup wins in a row with a 1-0 win over Rangers to make it 18 trophies won during the 2010s.

Christopher Jullien got the all-important goal and, after young Jeremie Frimpong was sent off, Fraser Forster produced a penalty save to keep his net intact, just as he did many times throughout the game in a Man of the Match performance.

DECEMBER FIXTURES
(Home fixtures in bold)

1	SPFL	4-1 v Ross County (Christie 2, Rogic, Johnston)
4	**SPFL**	**2-1 v Hamilton Accies (Christie, Brown)**
8	LC	1-0 v Rangers (Jullien)
12	UEL	0-2 v CFR Cluj
15	**SPFL**	**2-0 v Hibernian (Frimpong, Edouard)**
18	SPFL	2-0 v Hearts (Christie, Ntcham)
21	**SPFL**	**2-1 v Aberdeen (Jullien, Edouard)**
26	SPFL	2-1 v St Mirren (McGregor, Forrest)
29	**SPFL**	**1-2 v Rangers (Edouard)**

A makeshift Celtic team, with many players rested, lost 2-0 to Cluj in Romania in the final Group E game with the Celts now scheduled to play FC Copenhagen in the last 32-stage of the tournament in February.

In the league, there was a dramatic last-minute goal by Scott Brown for a vital 2-1 home win over Hamilton Accies, before both Edinburgh sides, Hibernian at home and Hearts at Tynecastle, were defeated 2-0 each. That was followed by two 2-1 victories, over Aberdeen at home and St Mirren away before the final game of the calendar year.

That produced another 2-1 scoreline, unfortunately in the favour of closest challengers, Rangers. That put the Ibrox club within two points of the Celts and they also had a game in hand – just what would happen after both clubs returned from their winter breaks in Dubai was anybody's guess.

THE TOP 3

	P	W	D	L	F	A	GD	Pts
Celtic	20	17	1	2	55	13	42	52
Rangers	19	16	2	1	53	11	42	50
Motherwell	21	12	1	8	33	27	6	37

JANUARY

CELTIC kicked-off the New Year and the defence of the Scottish Cup with a 2-1 win over Partick Thistle in Maryhill before returning to league duty with a 3-1 defeat of Kilmarnock on a trip to Rugby Park.

The first game of 2020 at Paradise saw a 3-0 win over Ross County while, the following day, Rangers made the trip to play bottom club, Hearts.

JANUARY FIXTURES
(Home fixtures in bold)

18	SC	2-1 v Partick Thistle (Griffiths, McGregor)
22	SPFL	3-1 v Kilmarnock (Edouard, Griffiths, Jullien)
25	**SPFL**	**3-0 v Ross County (McGregor, Edouard 2)**
29	SPFL	3-0 v St Johnstone (Ntcham, Forrest, Griffiths)

The Tynecastle club won 2-1 while Celtic followed up the 3-0 Ross County win with the same winning scoreline on a trip to McDiarmid Park to play St Johnstone.

The Hoops came through the truncated January schedule with four wins from four in two competitions while that two-point gap at the end of December had stretched to five after only three league games.

THE TOP 3

	P	W	D	L	F	A	GD	Pts
Celtic	**23**	**20**	**1**	**2**	**64**	**14**	**50**	**61**
Rangers	22	18	2	2	57	13	44	56
Motherwell	23	13	2	8	34	27	7	41

FEBRUARY

THE Celts went into the first game of the month knowing that they could increase their lead at the top of the table to six points after Aberdeen had drawn 0-0 at Ibrox the previous day – and the Hoops duly took advantage with a 4-1 away win at Hamilton Accies.

FEBRUARY FIXTURES

(Home fixtures in bold)

2	SPFL	4-1 v Hamilton Accies (Edouard 2, Jullien, Forrest)	
5	SPFL	4-0 v Motherwell (Edouard 2, Griffiths, McGregor)	
9	SC	3-0 v Clyde (Ntcham, Brown, Bayo)	
12	**SPFL**	**5-0 v Hearts (Ntcham, Jullien, McGregor, Christie, Simunovic)**	
16	SPFL	2-1 v Aberdeen (McGregor, Ajer)	
20	EL	1-1 v FC Copenhagen (Edouard)	
23	**SPFL**	**3-1 v Kilmarnock (Ajer, Edouard, Griffiths)**	
27	**EL**	**1-3 v FC Copenhagen (Edouard)**	

Lanarkshire was also the destination for the next league trip, and another four goals were scored, this time with no reply, at Motherwell.

Another Scottish Cup interlude followed with a 3-0 win over Clyde in Cumbernauld before Hearts visited on league duty and a sterling 5-0 Wednesday-night win with five different scorers ensued as the news drifted through from Rugby Park that Kilmarnock had beaten Rangers 2-1.

A 2-1 win over Aberdeen at Pittodrie kept the momentum going while the next title game was bookended by a 1-1 draw and 3-1 defeat by FC Copenhagen in the Europa League.

The disappointment of the European exit was tempered, though, by Celtic's standing in the league. The final 3-1 over Kilmarnock, that delivered five league wins out of five with 18 goals scored and only three against, came on the same night that Rangers dropped another two points, this time at St Johnstone - the gap was now 12 points, an increase of 10 points after only eight games.

THE TOP 3

	P	W	D	L	F	A	GD	Pts
Celtic	**28**	**25**	**1**	**2**	**82**	**17**	**65**	**76**
Rangers	27	20	4	3	63	18	45	64
Motherwell	28	13	3	12	36	36	0	42

THE 9-IN-A-ROW SEASON

MARCH

THE first day of March went as well for Celtic as the final day of February had gone badly for Rangers as the Ibrox side went out of the Scottish Cup by 1-0 to bottom club Hearts.

The Celts won by the same scoreline at St Johnstone thanks to a Ryan Christie goal in their quarter-final tie the following day.

Midweek saw a trip to play Livingston, where the Celts had lost 2-0 earlier in the season, and this time a 2-2 draw was the outcome.

MARCH FIXTURES
(Home fixtures in bold)

1	SC	1-0 v St Johnstone (Christie)
4	SPFL	2-2 v Livingston (McGregor, Rogic)
7	**SPFL**	**5-0 v St Mirren (Griffiths 3, Edouard, McGregor)**

The previous night, though, Hearts beat Hibernian 3-1 to crawl off the bottom of the table, leaving Hamilton Accies propping up the rest of the league. And while Celtic were drawing 2-2 at Livingston, bottom club Accies won 1-0 at Ibrox.

The Hoops, in what was to prove to be their final game, beat St Mirren 5-0 while the following day Rangers beat Ross County 1-0.

We didn't know it at the time, but football was over due to the Coronavirus outbreak. However, Celtic's scintillating form since returning from the winter break warm-weather training camp in Dubai saw them open up a 13-point lead at the top of the table.

The playing stats in the 10 league games played by both teams vying for the title since the turn of the year told their own story.

	P	W	D	L	F	A	GD	Pts
Celtic	10	9	1	0	30	6	24	28
Rangers	10	5	2	3	11	8	3	17

It was this sort of relentless match-winning tenacity that went a long way to resolving the issue of the destination of the title the following month.

THE TOP 3

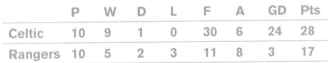

	P	W	D	L	F	A	GD	Pts
Celtic	30	26	2	2	89	19	70	80
Rangers	29	21	4	4	64	19	45	67
Motherwell	30	14	4	12	41	38	3	46

THE 9-IN-A-ROW SEASON

CHAMPIONS

APRIL/MAY

IT may not have been the title party that Hoops supporters had become familiar with over the previous decade, but it was nonetheless celebrated joyously by individuals and Celtic families all over the globe.

With the final league games played on the weekend of March 7, all other games from March, April and May were cancelled due to the Coronavirus outbreak and the lockdown that followed it.

Football, like so many other facets of everyday life took a backseat amid the many life-saving initiatives embraced in Scotland as key workers in many frontline jobs kept the country on an even keel.

Back in the football world, around lunchtime on Monday, May 18, the expected outcome arrived when it was announced that Celtic were indeed the SPFL champions for season 2019/20 – Nine-in-a-row was a reality.

The Celts of the 2010s had all helped to achieve what the great Jock Stein's team did between seasons 1965/66 and 1973/74 – win nine championships all in a row.

What makes both these sides stand out even more, though, was that they both delivered other silverware in abundance throughout their individual roads to those nine titles.

For a club to win Nine-in-a-row just once is an astounding achievement – to do it twice is way off the radar for most football fans.

The Celts of the 2010s had all helped to achieve what the great Jock Stein's team did between seasons 1965/66 and 1973/74 – win nine championships all in a row.

What makes both these sides stand out even more, though, was that they both delivered other silverware in abundance throughout their individual roads to those nine titles.

For a club to win Nine-in-a-row just once is an astounding achievement – to do it twice is way off the radar for most football fans.

SPFL LEAGUE TABLE 2019/20

	P	W	D	L	F	A	GD	Pts
Celtic	30	26	2	2	89	19	70	80
Rangers	29	21	4	4	64	19	45	67
Motherwell	30	14	4	12	41	38	3	46
Aberdeen	30	12	9	9	40	36	4	45
Livingston	30	10	9	11	42	49	2	39
Hibernian	30	9	10	11	42	49	-11	37
St Johnstone	29	8	12	9	28	46	-18	36
Kilmarnock	30	9	6	15	31	41	-10	33
St Mirren	30	7	8	15	24	41	-17	29
Ross County	30	7	8	15	29	60	-31	29
Hamilton Accies	30	6	9	15	30	50	-20	27
Hearts	30	4	11	15	31	52	-21	23

DECADE OF DOMINANCE
THE 2010s... MANAGERS

THE background story of the 2010s was the tale of three managers as far as Celtic are concerned as Neil Lennon, Ronny Deila and Brendan Rodgers have proved to be among the most successful in the club's history on a season to silverware basis.

Irishman, Neil Lennon, has, of course, bookended the silver-strewn success of the period and has racked up an amazing total of **NINE** trophy wins for the Celts over the piece. That includes no fewer than five championships, three Scottish Cups and one League Cup.

Following the first three titles of the current nine-in-a-row under Neil Lennon, it was the turn of Norwegian, Ronny Deila to come in, and he duly kept the silver conveyor belt flowing. In only two seasons, he delivered another two titles and the League Cup to the haul.

Next up was another Irishman in the shape of Brendan Rodgers, and it seemed he just didn't know how to lose when leading the Celts. There was a clean sweep of all the silverware as two titles, two Scottish Cups and the League Cup all took up residence in the Celtic Park trophy room for the duration.

Away from the Hoops during the decade, the trio of managers didn't do too badly either. While Celtic were painting Glasgow Green and White in the Invincible season, Neil Lennon was helping Hibernian do the same through in Edinburgh as the Easter Road side lifted the Championship. Before arriving at Celtic, Ronny Deila had already lifted the Norwegian Cup (2010) and the title (2013) with Stromsgodset. And, down south, in 2011 via the play-offs, Brendan Rodgers led Swansea to the Premier League – the first Welsh club to do so.

FLYING THE FLAG

IT may not have looked like a typical matchday outside Celtic Park on Sunday, August 2, 2020, and, of course, it wasn't.

This was the first competitive lockdown match at Celtic Park and even then, this wasn't just any old match – this was another Flag Day at Paradise and it wasn't any old Flag Day either, this was when eight successive Premiership flags fluttered in the breeze above Celtic's home waiting to be joined by the ninth.

While there may not have been the usual 60,000 inside Paradise cheering as the latest ninth title flag was unfurled, countless Celtic supporters throughout the world tuned in, logged on and set the volume controls to 10 as skipper, Scott Brown delivered the SPFL trophy to the centre-spot.

Paradise may have looked as peculiar for a matchday inside as it did outside, but once the referee's whistle blew, it was back to business as usual for the Celts.

An Odsonne Edouard hat-trick was added to by goals from Jeremie Frimpong and Patryk Klimala as the Hoops opened up their bid for a 10th successive title with a 5-1 win over Hamilton Accies.

PARADISE PROFILES

SCOTT BROWN

JAMES FORREST

VASILIS BARKAS

TOM ROGIC

NIR BITTON

LEIGH GRIFFITHS

CALLUM McGREGOR

RYAN CHRISTIE

ANTHONY RALSTON

KRISTOFFER AJER

OLIVIER NTCHAM

MIKEY JOHNSTON

ODSONNE EDOUARD

SCOTT BAIN

EWAN HENDERSON

CONOR HAZARD

KARAMOKO DEMBELE

CHRISTOPHER JULLIEN

LUCA CONNELL

HATEM ABD ELHAMED

DAVID TURNBULL

ISMAILA SORO

PATRYK KLIMALA

GREG TAYLOR

MOHAMED ELYOUNOUSSI

JEREMIE FRIMPONG

ALBIAN AJETI

SCOTT ROBERTSON

SCOTT BROWN

Position: Midfielder **Squad Number:** 8
D.O.B: 25/06/85 **Born:** Dunfermline, Scotland
Height: 5'10" **Signed:** 29/05/07
Debut: v Kilmarnock (h) 0-0, (SPL) 05/08/07
Previous Clubs: Hibernian

JAMES FORREST

Position: Winger **Squad Number:** 49
D.O.B: 07/07/91 **Born:** Prestwick, Scotland
Height: 5'9" **Signed:** 30/08/09
Debut: v Motherwell (h) 4-0, (SPL) 01/05/10
Previous Clubs: Celtic Youth

VASILIS BARKAS

Position: Goalkeeper **Squad Number:** 1
D.O.B: 30/05/94 **Born:** Zetten, Netherlands
Height: 6'5" **Signed:** 30/07/20
Debut: v Kilmarnock (a) 1-1, (SPFL) 09/08/20
Previous Clubs: AEK Athens, Atromitos

TOM ROGIC

Position: Midfielder **Squad Number:** 18
D.O.B: 16/12/92 **Born:** Griffith, Australia
Height: 6'2" **Signed:** 09/01/13
Debut: v Inverness Caley Thistle (a) 3-1, (SPL) 09/02/13
Previous Clubs: Central Coast Mariners, Belconnen
United, ANU FC

PARADISE PROFILES

NIR BITTON

Position: Midfielder **Squad Number:** 6
D.O.B: 30/10/91 **Born:** Ashdod, Israel
Height: 6'5" **Signed:** 30/08/13
Debut: v AC Milan (a) 0-2, (UCL) 18/09/13
Previous Clubs: FC Ashdod

LEIGH GRIFFITHS

Position: Striker **Squad Number:** 9
D.O.B: 20/08/90 **Born:** Edinburgh, Scotland
Height: 5'9" **Signed:** 31/01/14
Debut: v Aberdeen (a) 1-2, (SPFL) 08/02/14
Previous Clubs: Wolverhampton Wanderers,
Hibernian (loan), Dundee, Livingston

CALLUM McGREGOR

Position: Midfielder **Squad Number:** 42
D.O.B: 14/06/93 **Born:** Glasgow, Scotland
Height: 5'10"
Debut: v KR Reykjavik (a) 1-0, (UCL) 15/07/14
Previous Clubs: Notts County (loan)

RYAN CHRISTIE

Position: Midfielder **Squad Number:** 17
D.O.B: 22/02/95 **Born:** Inverness, Scotland
Height: 5'10" **Signed:** 01/09/15
Debut: v St Johnstone (h) 3-1, (SPFL) 23/01/16
Previous Clubs: Inverness Caledonian Thistle,
Aberdeen (loan)

ANTHONY RALSTON

Position: Defender **Squad Number:** 56
D.O.B: 16/11/98 **Born:** Bellshill, Scotland
Height: 5'11" **Debut:** v St Johnstone (a) 1-2,
(SPFL) 11/05/16
Previous Clubs: Dundee Utd (loan)

KRISTOFFER AJER

Position: Midfielder **Squad Number:** 35
D.O.B: 17/04/98 **Born:** Raelingen, Norway
Height: 6' 4" **Signed:** 17/02/16
Debut: v Lincoln Red Imps (h) 3-0, (UCL) 20/07/16
Previous Clubs: IK Start, Kilmarnock (loan)

OLIVIER NTCHAM

Position: Midfielder **Squad Number:** 21
D.O.B: 09/02/96 **Born:** Longjumeau, France
Height: 5' 9" **Signed:** 12/07/17
Debut: v Linfield (h) 4-0, (UCL) 19/07/17
Previous Clubs: Genoa (loan), Manchester City

MIKEY JOHNSTON

Position: Striker **Squad Number:** 19
D.O.B: 19/04/99 **Born:** Glasgow, Scotland
Height: 5' 10"
Debut: v St Johnstone (h) 4-1, (SPFL) 06/05/17
Previous Clubs: Celtic Youth

PARADISE PROFILES

ODSONNE EDOUARD

Position: Striker **Squad Number:** 22
D.O.B: 16/01/98 **Born:** Kourou, French Guiana
Height: 6'1" **Signed:** 31/08/17
Debut: v Hamilton Accies (a) 4-1, (SPFL) 08/09/17
Previous Clubs: Toulouse (loan), Paris Saint-Germain

SCOTT BAIN

Position: Goalkeeper **Squad Number:** 29
D.O.B: 22/11/91 **Born:** Edinburgh, Scotland
Height: 6'0" **Signed:** 31/01/18
Debut: v Rangers (a) 3-2, (SPFL) 11/03/18
Previous Clubs: Hibernian (loan), Dundee, Alloa Athletic, Elgin City (loan), Aberdeen

EWAN HENDERSON

Position: Midfielder **Squad Number:** 52
D.O.B: 27/03/2000 **Born:** Edinburgh, Scotland
Height: 5'9" **Signed:** 01/08/17
Debut: v Kilmarnock (h) 0-0, (SPFL) 09/05/18
Previous Clubs: Celtic Youth

CONOR HAZARD

Position: Goalkeeper **Squad Number:** 65
D.O.B: 05/03/98 **Born:** Downpatrick, Ireland
Height: 6' 5" **Signed:** 20/05/14
Debut: n/a
Previous Clubs: Celtic Youth

KARAMOKO DEMBELE

Position: Midfielder **Squad Number:** 77
D.O.B: 22/02/03 **Born:** London, England
Height: 5'3"
Debut: v Hearts (h) 2-1, (SPFL) 19/5/19
Previous Clubs: Celtic Youth

CHRISTOPHER JULLIEN

Position: Defender **Squad Number:** 2
D.O.B: 22/03/93 **Born:** Lagny-sur-Marne, France
Height: 6'5" **Signed:** 28/06/19
Debut: v Nomme Kalju (a) 2-0, (UCL) 30/07/19
Previous Clubs: Toulouse, Dijon (loan), SC Freiburg, Auxerre

LUCA CONNELL

Position: Midfielder **Squad Number:** 28
D.O.B: 20/04/01 **Born:** Liverpool, England
Height: 5'10" **Signed:** 29/06/19
Debut: n/a
Previous Clubs: Bolton Wanderers

HATEM ABD ELHAMED

Position: Defender **Squad Number:** 33
D.O.B: 18/03/91 **Born:** Kafr Manda, Israel
Height: 6'1" **Signed:** 24/07/19
Debut: v St Johnstone (h) 7-0, (SFPL) 03/08/19
Previous Clubs: Hapoel Be'er Sheva, FC Ashdod (loan), Gent,
Dinamo Bucharest (loan), FC Ashdod, Charleroi (loan), Maccabi Tel Aviv

PARADISE PROFILES

DAVID TURNBULL

Position: Midfielder **Squad Number:** 14
D.O.B: 10/07/1999 **Born:** Carluke, Scotland
Height: 6'1" **Signed:** 27/08/20
Debut: v n/a
Previous Clubs: Motherwell

ISMAILA SORO

Position: Midfielder **Squad Number:** 12
D.O.B: 07/05/98 **Born:** Yakasse-Me, Ivory Coast
Height: 5'8" **Signed:** 27/01/20
Debut: v N/A
Previous Clubs: Bnei Yehuda, Gomel, Saxan

PATRYK KLIMALA

Position: Striker **Squad Number:** 11
D.O.B: 05/08/98 **Born:** Swidnica, Poland
Height: 6'0" **Signed:** 14/01/20
Debut: v Partick Thistle (a) 2-1, (Scottish Cup) 18/01/20
Previous Clubs: Wigry Suwalki (loan), Jagiellona Bialystok,
Lechia Dzierzoniow (loan), Legia Warsaw

GREG TAYLOR

Position: Defender **Squad Number:** 3
D.O.B: 05/11/1997 **Born:** Greenock, Scotland
Height: 5'8" **Signed:** 02/09/19
Debut: v St Mirren (h) 2-0, (SPFL) 30/10/19
Previous Clubs: Kilmarnock

MOHAMED ELYOUNOUSSI

Position: Forward **Squad Number:** 27
D.O.B: 04/08/1994 **Born:** Al Hoceima, Morocco
Height: 5'10" **Signed:** 30/08/19
Debut: v Hamilton Accies (a) 1-0, (SPFL) 14/09/19
Previous Clubs: Southampton, Basel, Molde, Sarpsborg 08

JEREMIE FRIMPONG

Position: Defender **Squad Number:** 30
D.O.B: 10/12/2000 **Born:** Amsterdam, Netherlands
Height: 5'7" **Signed:** 02/09/19
Debut: v Partick Thistle (h) 5-0, (LC) 25/09/19
Previous Clubs: Manchester City Youth

ALBIAN AJETI

Position: Forward **Squad Number:** 10
D.O.B: 26/02/1997 **Born:** Basel, Switzerland
Height: 6'0" **Signed:** 13/08/20
Debut: v KR Reykjavik (h), 6-0, (UCL) 18/08/20
Previous Clubs: West Ham, Basel, St Gallen, FC Ausburg, Basel

SCOTT ROBERTSON

Position: Midfielder **Squad Number:** 41
D.O.B: 27/07/2001 **Born:** Lenzie, Scotland
Height: 5'9" **Signed:** 24/07/19
Debut: v CFR Cluj (a) 0-2, (EL) 12/12/19
Previous Clubs: Celtic Youth

GHIRL POWER

THE women's game was affected just as much as men's football and every other sport by the Coronavirus pandemic.

However, great strides had been made by Celtic FC Women going into the season with the Ghirls turning professional, new sponsorship deals and new signings bolstering a squad that was already on a high.

The feel-good factor came from the Ghirls' performances on the pitch, with skipper, Kelly Clark leading the team to some sparkling results at the end of the 2019 season – and that was to carry on into the start of the curtailed 2020 term.

Indeed, long-term champions, Glasgow City had been defeated 4-1 as 2019 edged to a close, and, just to prove that wasn't a fluke, the Ghirls then defeated the UEFA Champions League quarter-finalists 2-1 in the first league outing of the disrupted 2020 campaign.

That game at their K-Park home in East Kilbride was also the first SWPL match with new manager, Fran Alonso in charge, and the Spaniard has opened transfer doors not only in his Spanish homeland, but elsewhere as well.

Before the start of the truncated 2020 season, Keeva Keenan from Ireland and Josie Giard from Germany were the only non-Scots in the side. However, the squad was then strengthened and added to with experienced players from Spain, as well as the United States and down south in England.

It's all part of the drive towards regular silverware at Celtic Park not being purely the domain of the men's team.

DECADE OF DOMINANCE
THE 2010s... PLAYERS

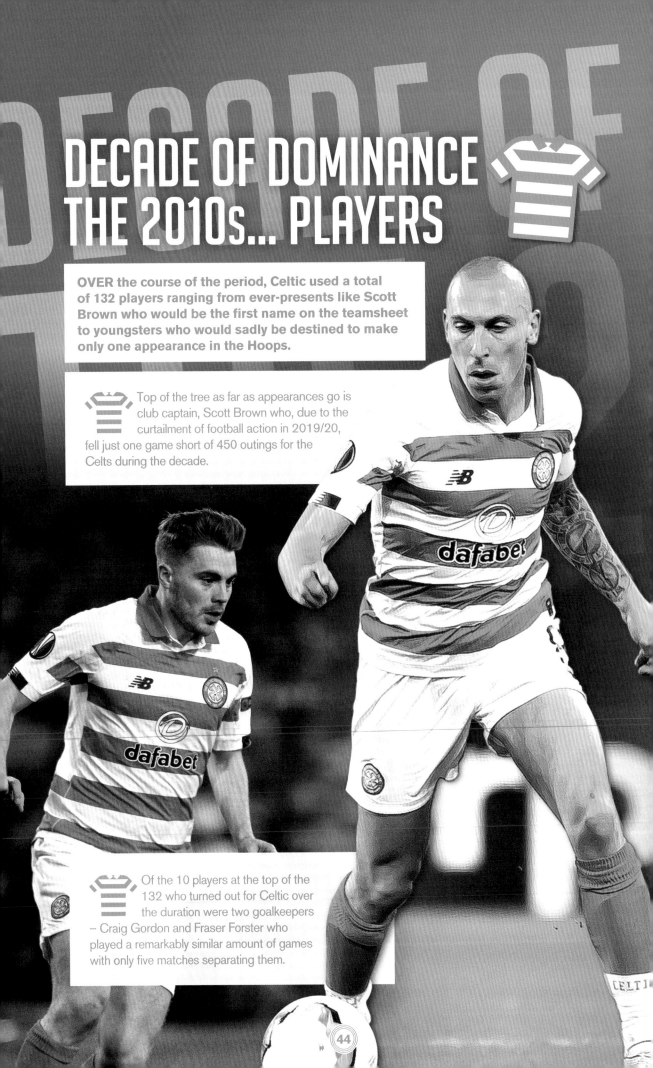

OVER the course of the period, Celtic used a total of 132 players ranging from ever-presents like Scott Brown who would be the first name on the teamsheet to youngsters who would sadly be destined to make only one appearance in the Hoops.

Top of the tree as far as appearances go is club captain, Scott Brown who, due to the curtailment of football action in 2019/20, fell just one game short of 450 outings for the Celts during the decade.

Of the 10 players at the top of the 132 who turned out for Celtic over the duration were two goalkeepers – Craig Gordon and Fraser Forster who played a remarkably similar amount of games with only five matches separating them.

TOP 10 APPEARANCES

1.	SCOTT BROWN	449
2.	JAMES FORREST	391
3.	CALLUM McGREGOR	275
4.	MIKAEL LUSTIG	274
5.	EMILIO IZAGUIRRE	271
6.	CRAIG GORDON	242
7.	FRASER FORSTER	237
8.	LEIGH GRIFFITHS	232
9.	KRIS COMMONS	227
10.	CHARLIE MULGREW	208

Celtic's Top 10 for the decade have made 2,806 appearances over the course of the decade and five of the 10 are still with the club.

While Scott Brown is at the top, spare a thought for players such as Lewis Toshney, Richie Towell and Paul George who are among those who made only one appearance from the substitutes' bench during the timescale.

The longevity of players in football has a natural order with goalkeepers, defenders and defensive midfielders generally having longer careers in that sequence. That shows with only one out-and-out striker, Leigh Griffiths in the Top 10, although goal-getters like James Forrest and Callum McGregor are well up the pecking order.

GUESS WHO?

A

B

C

D

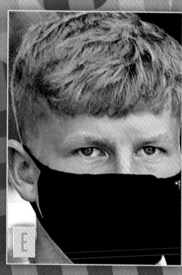

E

F

G

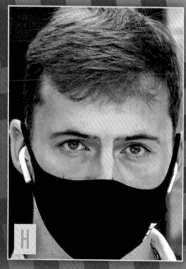

H

9-IN-A-ROW QUIZ

CAN you come up with the answers in this quiz of nine posers? There is one question for each of the nine-in-a-row years.

1. **2011/12:** Who was Celtic's top league scorer in this season?

2. **2012/13:** Which two goalkeepers played for Celtic in this league campaign?

3. **2013/14:** What did this season's clincher have in common with the previous two?

4. **2014/15:** On what day of the week was the title clinched?

5. **2015/16:** In the final game, what player made his debut and scored with his very first touch at the age of 16 years and 71 days to break two club records?

6. **2016/17:** Who were the visitors on trophy presentation day when Celtic completed he full league campaign unbeaten?

7. **2017/18:** What was the score when the Hoops clinched the title this season?

8. **2018/19:** Which Celtic legend presented the SPFL trophy at the end of the campaign?

9. **2019/20:** Winning the league meant Celtic had won how many domestic trophies in a row?

Answers on pages 62/63.

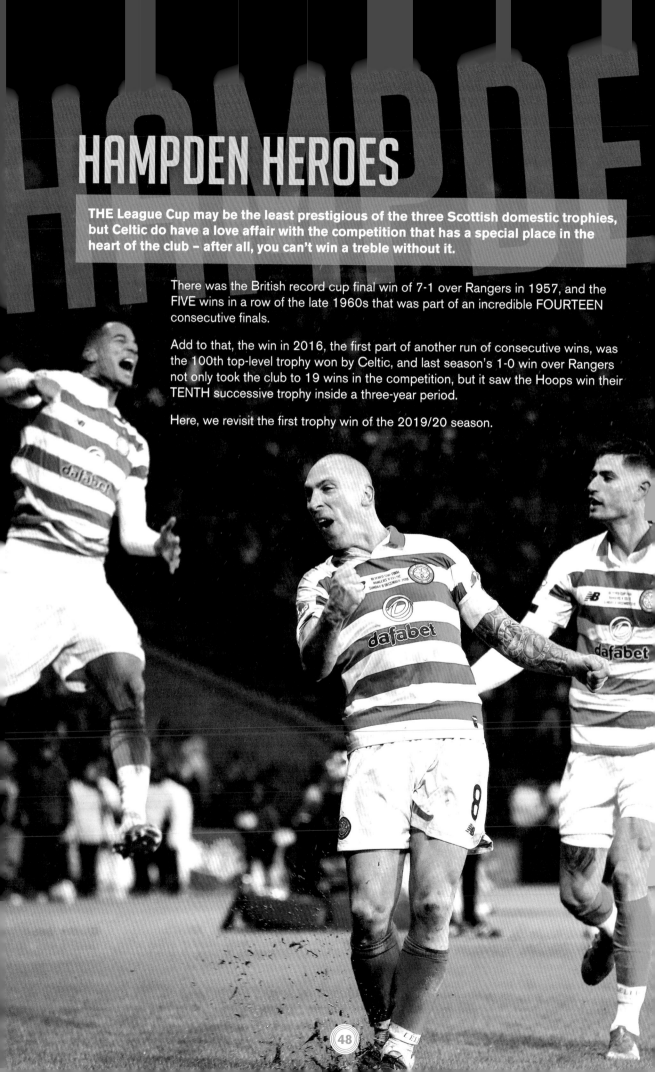

HAMPDEN HEROES

THE League Cup may be the least prestigious of the three Scottish domestic trophies, but Celtic do have a love affair with the competition that has a special place in the heart of the club – after all, you can't win a treble without it.

There was the British record cup final win of 7-1 over Rangers in 1957, and the FIVE wins in a row of the late 1960s that was part of an incredible FOURTEEN consecutive finals.

Add to that, the win in 2016, the first part of another run of consecutive wins, was the 100th top-level trophy won by Celtic, and last season's 1-0 win over Rangers not only took the club to 19 wins in the competition, but it saw the Hoops win their TENTH successive trophy inside a three-year period.

Here, we revisit the first trophy win of the 2019/20 season.

LEAGUE CUP FINAL SUNDAY, DECEMBER 8, 2019 HAMPDEN PARK, GLASGOW
CELTIC... 1 [JULLIEN 60] RANGERS... 0

A TEN-man Celtic side came out on top in a hard-fought Glasgow derby League Cup final to win 1-0 and clinch yet another crucial piece of silverware.

Neil Lennon brought on Odsonne Edouard shortly after the restart and the Frenchman was cynically chopped down out on the wing. It proved to be a costly mistake for Rangers.

Ryan Christie swung in the free-kick and Christopher Jullien side-footed the ball in from close-range in front of the Celtic fans.

Celtic were dealt a blow shortly after when Alfredo Morelos went down in the box under a challenge from Jeremie Frimpong. The referee issued a straight red card and awarded a penalty. The Columbian stepped up but he was no match for Fraser Forster who dived low to his right to make the all-important save.

The Hoops fans erupted in joy as the final whistle blew at a rain-soaked Hampden, confirming the Celts as the League Cup winners for a fourth consecutive year, a feat only previously achieved by Jock Stein's Celtic side.

CELTIC: Forster, Frimpong, Jullien, Ajer, Hayes, Brown, McGregor, Forrest (Bitton 66), Christie, Elyounoussi (Johnston 46), Morgan (Edouard 58)

Subs: Gordon, Rogic, Ntcham, Bolingoli

RANGERS: McGregor, Tavernier, Goldson, Helander (Katic 83), Barisic, Kamara (Defoe 71), Jack, Aribo (Barker 74), Arfield, Kent, Morelos.

Subs: Foderingham, Ojo, Stewart, Flanagan

WINNER WORDS: Christopher Jullien

Every time I go up, I'm looking to head the ball, but I didn't think it would come through to me. When I saw it sit up for me I just reacted and it went in. I can't describe the moment. I knew when it went in that there was a lot of time left in the game. I knew I couldn't get carried away because I had to be really focused for the time left in the game. I'm really happy that goal got us the win.

This is my first trophy and to do it at a club with these players, staff and fans is just unbelievable. This goal is the one that means the most to me. The one against Lazio was huge in my career but this one is the best because it gave me my trophy. It's for sure the best day of my life in terms of what I've achieved in football.

TROPHY ON TOUR

THE Coronavirus outbreak had a far more serious impact on people's lives than merely cancelling some football games, but it did rob Celtic players and supporters of the now annual ritual of the trophy presentation and parade of the silverware at Paradise.

Not to be outdone though, the club managed to transport the trophy on a little trip around the Central Belt visiting the homes of nine lucky Celts so they could at least get their hands on the trophy.

Here we revisit that tour, starting with Hoops skipper, Scott Brown at his spiritual home of Celtic Park, and end, appropriately, with No.9, Leigh Griffiths.

EDOUARD

CHRISTIE

FORREST

SPFL LEAGUE TABLE 2019/20

	P	W	D	L	F	A	GD	Pts
Celtic	30	26	2	2	89	19	70	80
Rangers	29	21	4	4	64	19	45	67
Motherwell	30	14	4	12	41	38	3	46
Aberdeen	30	12	9	9	40	36	4	45
Livingston	30	10	9	11	41	39	2	39
Hibernian	30	9	10	11	42	49	-7	37
St Johnstone	29	8	12	9	28	46	-18	36
Kilmarnock	30	9	6	15	31	41	-10	33
St Mirren	30	7	8	15	24	41	-17	29
Ross County	30	7	8	15	29	60	-31	29
Hamilton Accies	30	6	9	15	30	50	-20	27
Hearts	30	4	11	15	31	52	-21	23

TITLE TRAVEL TEST

WHEN Jock Stein's all-conquering Celts of the late 1960s and early '70s achieved the first nine-in-a-row, not one of the titles was clinched at Celtic Park.

This time around, only four of the championships were sealed in games away from Paradise. Can you match up the season with the winning venue?

2011/12:

2013/14:

2016/17:

2018/19:

Tynecastle

Rugby Park

Firhill

Pittodrie

LEAGUE CUP FINAL – BEFORE AND AFTER

THESE two photographs show Hoops manager, Neil Lennon at the start and the finish of the League Cup final action.

Can you help him get from pre-match hopes to post-match celebrations?

SPOT THE DIFFERENCE

THERE are 10 differences between these two photographs that feature Kristoffer Ajer heading goalwards against Hamilton Accies. The first one has been circled, but can you spot the rest?

Answers on pages 62/63.

DECADE OF DOMINANCE THE 2010s... ANNUALS

OVER the past 10 years or so there have been many highs and thankfully few lows in following the Hoops in their quest for silverware, and the Celtic Annual has been there all the way with the team.

The front covers have featured many different players over the course of the decade and a few different versions of the world-famous green and white hoops have also been highlighted with each new generation of Celtic fans discovering the delights of the latest annual on Christmas morning.

Here we take a look at the previous Celtic Annual front covers from our Decade of Dominance.

The Official **CELTIC FOOTBALL CLUB** Annual 2010

THE OFFICIAL **CELTIC FC** ANNUAL 2011

The Official **CELTIC** Annual 2012

The Official **CELTIC** Annual -2013-

THE OFFICI **CELTI** ANNUAL 201

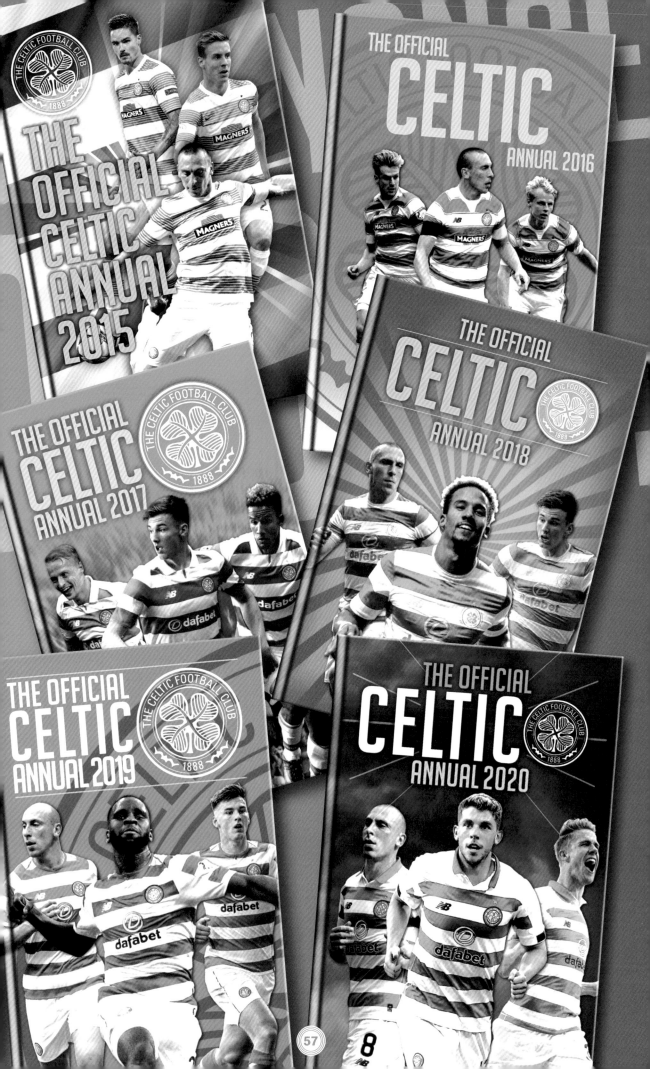

THE OFFICIAL CELTIC ANNUAL 2015

THE OFFICIAL CELTIC ANNUAL 2016

THE OFFICIAL CELTIC ANNUAL 2017

THE OFFICIAL CELTIC ANNUAL 2018

THE OFFICIAL CELTIC ANNUAL 2019

THE OFFICIAL CELTIC ANNUAL 2020

DECADE OF DOMINANCE THE 2010s... GOALS AND SCORERS

OVER the seasons featured in the 2010s, the Hoops scored no fewer than 1,278 goals in all competitions as the trophies rolled in.

Top of the tree in the goalscoring stakes is Celtic's current No.9, sharpshooter, Leigh Griffiths who clocked in with an amazing 115 goals over the piece.

With two spots (No.6 and No.9) tied by two players, this means 12 Celts feature in the Top 10 places and, such is the potency of Celtic's driving attack from defence and midfield, only half of that number could be considered as out-and-out strikers.

The most goal-laden season of the decade was the 2016/17 Invincible season as the Hoops battered in no fewer than 150 goals – 106 in the league, 11 in the League Cup, 17 in the Scottish Cup and 16 in Europe.

Top Bhoy, Leigh Griffiths got 18 of his 115 goals in the Invincible season, while his best term was the previous campaign when he rammed home an astounding 40 goals in only 51 games.

DOMINANCE

TOP 10 SCORERS

1.	LEIGH GRIFFITHS	115
2.	KRIS COMMONS	91
3.	JAMES FORREST	87
4.	GARY HOOPER	82
5.	ANTHONY STOKES	77
6.	ODSONNE EDOUARD/ SCOTT SINCLAIR	62
7.	MOUSSA DEMBELE	51
8.	CALLUM McGREGOR	44
9.	TOM ROGIC/ GEORGIOS SAMARAS	38
10.	SCOTT BROWN	35

To prove the fact that Celtic score from all areas, easing in at No.10 is none other than super-skipper, Scott Brown who props up the rest of the table with a more than healthy 35 goals.

Opposition clubs should beware as **SIX** of the top scorers on the list started season 2020/21 with the club – Leigh Griffiths, James Forrest, Odsonne Edouard, Callum McGregor, Tom Rogic and Scott Brown.

DECADE OF DOMINANCE
THE 2010s... TROPHIES

IF one image sums up the 2010s for Celtic, it must be that of Scott Brown raising aloft the silverware before passing the trophy along to his celebrating team-mates – it happened that often it's a wonder his arms didn't get sore.

There were, of course, **NINE** consecutive league titles lifted over the course of the period as the club equalled the feat of Jock Stein's Celts of half-a-century earlier.

Of the five Scottish Cup wins, the most recent three were consecutive wins as part of the Treble Treble.

60

WINNERS 2017

WINNERS 2018

BETFRED CUP

LEAGUE TITLE
2011/12, 2012/13, 2013/14, 2014/15, 2015/16, 2016/17, 2017/18, 2018/19, 2019/20

SCOTTISH CUP
2010/11, 2012/13, 2016/17, 2017/18, 2018/19

LEAGUE CUP
2014/15, 2016/17, 2017/18, 2018/19, 2019/20

The Hoops also won **FOUR** successive League Cups and didn't lose a single goal in any of the five winning finals with scores of 2-0 (Dundee United), 3-0 (Aberdeen), 2-0 (Motherwell), 1-0 (Aberdeen) and 1-0 (Rangers).

With 39 winning finals, Celtic are the most successful side in the Scottish Cup.

ANSWERS

PAGE 46: GUESS WHO?

A. Chris Jullien
B. Vasilias Barkas
C. Karamoko Dembele
D. Hatem Elhamed
E. Scott Robertson
F. Scott Brown
G. Ryan Christie
H. Conor Hazard

PAGE 47: NINE-IN-A-ROW QUIZ

1. 2011/12: Gary Hooper with 24 goals.
2. 2012/13: Fraser Forster and Lukasz Zaluska.
3. 2013/14: In all three games, goals were scored in the 90th minute.
4. 2014/15: Celtic beat Dundee 5-0 on a Friday night and Aberdeen lost the following day.
5. 2015/16: Jack Aitchison.
6. 2016/17: Celtic beat Hearts 2-0.
7. 2017/18: Celtic beat Rangers 5-0 at Paradise to claim the championship.
8. 2018/19: Paul McStay.
9. 2019/20: Eleven.

PAGE 54: TITLE TRAVEL TEST

2011/12: Rugby Park
2013/14: Firhill
2016/17: Tynecastle
2018/19: Pittodrie

9 CHAMPIONS